nancie m. wiseman

start with a
sweatshirt

sew a stylish jacket

Martingale®
& C O M P A N Y

dedication

To my husband's daughters, their husbands, and children:
Sharon, Rich, granddaughter Nicole; Karen, Ron, and
grandson Tanner. Thanks for putting your arms around me.

Start with a Sweatshirt: Sew a Stylish Jacket
© 2008 by Nancie M. Wiseman

Martingale® & COMPANY

That Patchwork Place® is an imprint of
Martingale & Company®.

Martingale & Company
20205 144th Ave. NE
Woodinville, WA 98072-8478 USA
www.martingale-pub.com

Printed in China
13 12 11 10 09 08   8 7 6 5 4 3 2 1

The information in this book is presented in good faith, but
no warranty is given nor results guaranteed. Since Martingale
& Company has no control over choice of materials or
procedures, the company assumes no responsibility for the
use of this information.

Library of Congress Cataloging-in-Publication Data
Library of Congress Control Number: 2008037461

ISBN: 978-1-56477-867-3

credits

President & CEO   Tom Wierzbicki
Editorial Director   Mary V. Green
Managing Editor   Tina Cook
Technical Editor   Dawn Anderson
Copy Editor   Marcy Heffernan
Design Director   Stan Green
Production Manager   Regina Girard
Illustrator   Robin Strobel
Cover & Text Designer   Shelly Garrison
Photographer   Brent Kane

mission statement

Dedicated to providing quality products
and service to inspire creativity.

contents

introduction   4

general instructions   5

projects

mandarin   8

spring trees   14

pure and simple black and white   20

pickin' daisies   24

tucks on the diagonal   28

about the author   back cover

introduction

I love making jackets from sweatshirts! It all began for me when I started adding bands and zippers to sweatshirts, and then one day I wondered, "Why can't I just cover the whole sweatshirt with fabric?"

I experimented by cutting up sweatshirts and finding the best way to put them back together. There were many pieces to the puzzle I needed to figure out, including where and when to cut, sew, quilt, and embellish. I sewed seams in the sweatshirt fabric itself and also sewed seams in the sweatshirt layered with cotton fabric. I was afraid the sweatshirt would lose its shape. It didn't.

In fact nothing happened that made continuing seem like a bad idea. I wanted the sweatshirt jackets to have some couture style. I didn't want them to look like quilts, but instead be dressy and classy. I don't think the jackets even slightly resemble sweatshirts anymore, except for the fact that they are still as warm, cozy, and comfortable as a sweatshirt. Not to mention, these jackets are more fun to wear.

I was ready to roll with my ideas. I haunted quilt shops and found glorious fabrics that I knew would work just right with the ideas that were swirling around in my head. Then I found a great source for sweatshirts. My sewing machine hummed, and I was off on a great adventure.

None of the jackets are hard to make. The illustrations and instructions will guide you through the process. I know you'll have a great time picking the fabric and finding the perfect color sweatshirt.

It has been a great pleasure for me to work on and write this book. I'm known in the fiber world as a knitter and crocheter. Writing this book has been a great introduction for me to the world of quilting.

general instructions

The information in this section covers basic supplies needed and offers instructions for deconstructing your sweatshirt, applying interfacing, and binding. Follow the instructions for each project, referring back to this section as necessary.

choosing a sweatshirt

For each jacket you will need a prewashed sweatshirt in your size or a little larger. The dimensions of the finished jacket will be smaller than the original sweatshirt due to seaming and quilting, so in some cases you may need to purchase a sweatshirt larger than you normally wear. The reduction in size varies with each project, so refer to the project materials for guidance in selecting a size.

Also keep in mind that every brand of sweatshirt varies in its measurements. Sweatshirts normally have a generous amount of wearing ease, so the jackets in this book are generally loose fitting through the body. The Mandarin jacket on page 8 has the closest fit. It is possible to reduce the amount of ease slightly around the body if desired by placing the buttons further from the front opening, so the jacket front pieces overlap slightly. For jackets with long sleeves, be sure to select a sweatshirt brand that will provide you with a sleeve of adequate length once the sleeve band is cut off. You will need the sleeve to reach the desired finished sleeve length plus ½" to 1" extra to allow for the amount removed by the armhole seam when the sleeve is stitched into the jacket.

If you can't find the type or color of sweatshirt you like locally, I recommend www.jiffyshirts.com for online ordering. Do not use a sweatshirt with raglan sleeves.

APPROXIMATE BUST MEASUREMENT OF FINISHED JACKET					
Small	Medium	Large	XL	2XL	3XL
34"	38"	44"	48"	54"	58"

Determine which side of the sweatshirt you would like to line the inside of the jacket—the smooth side (right side) or the fuzzy side (wrong side). The Mandarin jacket is made using the smooth side as the lining and the remaining projects give instructions for using the fuzzy side as the lining. If you choose to use a side other than what was used in the project instructions, remember to apply the interfacing to the side of the sweatshirt front that is not intended as lining.

selecting fabrics

Choose 100%-cotton quilting fabrics to transform your sweatshirt into a quilted jacket. Prewash the fabrics before cutting the jacket pieces to prevent excess shrinkage in the finished jacket. Press the fabric before cutting.

other supplies

- Medium-weight fusible interfacing
- Thread to match the jacket fabrics
- Thread to match the sweatshirt
- Bodkin or safety pin for turning bias tubes right side out
- Colored chalk or fabric-marking pen that will show both on your sweatshirt and through the interfacing when fused to the sweatshirt front
- Quilter's safety pins
- Rotary cutter and cutting mat
- Ruler at least 3½" wide x 24" long
- Sharp scissors

deconstructing the sweatshirt

Before you can begin creating your jacket, you'll need to deconstruct your sweatshirt.

1. Cut off the bottom band and the sleeve bands, cutting just above any top stitching. *Do not* cut the neckband off until instructed to do so in the project instructions.

2. If the project instructions call for a side seam, lay the sweatshirt out on a flat surface and press folds to indicate where the side seams would be on both sides of the sweatshirt body. Take care to align the pressed side seam with the sleeve seam at the underarm to create one continuous seam line. Cut the sides open up to the underarm seam.

3. Use a safety pin to mark each sleeve where it meets the shoulder seam and label the left and right sleeves with chalk or a fabric pen. Cut off the seam allowances around the sleeve seam along the seam line and remove the sleeves. Open the sleeve seam by turning the sleeve inside out and cutting off the seam allowances on the seam line. Set the sleeves aside.

4. Cut the shoulder seam and neckline as directed in your project instructions.

interfacing and prepping the sweatshirt

1. Mark the neck and front opening lines on the sweatshirt front as directed in the project instructions using a bright-colored fabric-marking pen that will show through the interfacing.

2. Cut a piece of medium-weight fusible interfacing to cover 3" on either side of the neck across both shoulders and the length of the sweatshirt front.

3. Following the manufacturer's instructions, fuse the interfacing to the sweatshirt front, covering the neckline and front markings; let cool. Remark the neck and front opening lines if necessary. Cut along the marked cutting lines, cutting through any excess interfacing at the ends of the lines. Trim away any excess interfacing.

binding

The jacket edges and some of the sleeves are finished with bias binding. The binding width is 2", 2½", or 3", depending on the individual jacket. Refer to the project instructions to find the width for each jacket.

The binding is cut from a tube of fabric that is made from a fabric square. The chart above right will help you determine what size of fabric square to cut in order to create a fabric tube that will yield the required length bias strips. The project instructions will list the approximate length of the bias strip needed for each jacket.

FABRIC REQUIREMENTS FOR BIAS BINDING			
Length of Binding	Size of Fabric Square Needed		
	For 2" strips	For 2½" strips	For 3" strips
150"	19" x 19"	21" x 21"	23" x 23"
180"	20" x 20"	23" x 23"	25" x 25"
210"	22" x 22"	24" x 24"	26" x 26"
240"	23" x 23"	26" x 26"	38" x 38"
280"	25" x 25"	28" x 28"	31" x 31"

bias strips

1. Refer to the project instructions to determine the approximate length of bias binding needed for the project. Look for the number closest to that in the chart above, round up, and cut a fabric square to the size indicated for that length of bias. Draw lines on the square with chalk or a marking pen as shown.

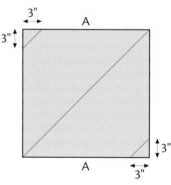

2. Cut on the diagonal marked lines. Discard the corner triangles.

3. Sew the two edges marked A (in the illustration above) right sides together with a ¼" seam allowance. Press the seam allowance open. Using a marking pen or chalk and a ruler, draw lines the length of the fabric, spacing them as specified in the project instructions.

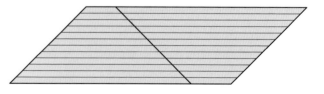

4. Cut along the first marked line at one end of the binding fabric for about 6". Fold the short ends of the fabric right sides together, offsetting the seam the width of the bias strip as shown, and stitch. Press the seam allowance open.

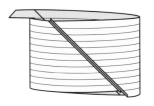

5. Using a pair of scissors, ontinue cutting along the marked line to create a continuous strip of bias binding.

how to attach bias binding

1. Fold the binding strip in half lengthwise, wrong sides together, and press.

2. Using ¼" seam allowance and leaving the first 10" of binding unstitched, stitch the binding, raw edges aligned, to the edge of the jacket, starting at either the lower edge of the jacket back or a side seam. For jackets with mitered corners, stop stitching ¼" from the corner and backstitch. Create mitered corners following steps 3 and 4. If the jacket doesn't have mitered corners, skip to step 5.

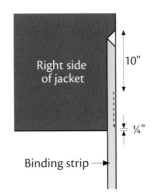

3. Clip the thread and remove the jacket from the sewing machine. Turn the jacket so you will be ready to stitch down the next side. Fold the binding up and away from you; finger-press the 45° angle that was created at the fold.

4. Fold the binding back down so it is even with the side edge of the jacket. The top fold should align with the edge of the jacket that is at the top. Begin stitching ¼" away from the fold and backstitch to secure the stitching.

5. Continue to apply binding around all the jacket edges until you are 10" from the starting point. Remove the jacket from the sewing machine. Fold the unsewn binding ends back on themselves so the folds meet in the middle; finger-press the folds.

6. Unfold both ends of the binding and overlap them, right sides together, matching the centers of the pressed folds. Pin and draw a diagonal line through the center of the X as shown. Stitch on the marked line and trim ¼" from the stitching. Finish stitching the binding to the jacket.

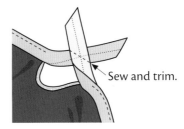

Sew and trim.

7. Fold the binding over the raw edges of the jacket so it just covers the machine stitching on the inside, and pin. Hand stitch the binding to the inside of the jacket with matching thread. Hand stitch any mitered corners in place.

Inside of jacket

mandarin

This jacket features center front knot-and-loop closures with replica Chinese coin button accents. The front pockets are nearly invisible on the front of the jacket except for the bias-bound upper edges. Cuffs add detail to the sleeves.

materials

Fabric quantities are listed by the size of the sweatshirt. Purchase a sweatshirt one size larger than you'd normally wear. For example, a size Large sweatshirt becomes a size Medium jacket. This jacket fits fairly close to the body without much ease, so if you want it roomier or are between sizes, you may want to start with a sweatshirt that has a generous amount of wearing ease. This jacket has long sleeves. Refer to "Choosing a Sweatshirt" on page 5 for guidance in selecting the appropriate size and sleeve length.

	Medium	Large	XL	2XL	3XL
Turquoise floral (main color—MC)	1⅝ yards	1⅝ yards	1⅞ yards	1⅞ yards	1⅞ yards
Turquoise small-scale floral (A)	¾ yard	¾ yard	1 yard	1 yard	1 yard
Pink floral (B)	⅝ yard	⅝ yard	¾ yard	¾ yard	¾ yard
Turquoise spatter print (C)	¾ yard	¾ yard	1 yard	1 yard	1 yard
Green leaf print (D)	½ yard	½ yard	¾ yard	¾ yard	¾ yard
Green batik (E)	⅜ yard	⅜ yard	⅝ yard	⅝ yard	⅝ yard
Medium-weight fusible interfacing	⅞ yard	⅞ yard	1 yard	1 yard	1 yard
Additional supplies	Sweatshirt Other supplies listed on page 5 6 replica Chinese coins (www.firemountaingems.com) Computer CD for template				

cutting

From the turquoise floral, cut:

4 strips (or more, depending on the sweatshirt size), 4½" x 42"

1 bias strip, 2" x 8"

2½"-wide bias strips (enough to go around the edges of the jacket and sleeves plus 10" for mitered corners and finishing—about 155" to 185"). See "Binding" on page 6.

From the turquoise small-scale floral *and* the turquoise spatter print, cut:

4 strips (or more, depending on the sweatshirt size), 4½" x 42"

From the pink floral, cut:

3 strips (or more, depending on the sweatshirt size), 4½" x 42"

1 bias strip, 2" x 8"

From the green leaf print, cut:

3 strips (or more, depending on the sweatshirt size), 4½" x 42"

From the green batik, cut:

2 strips (or more, depending on the sweatshirt size), 4½" x 42"

cutting segments

Using the pieced fabric illustrations on pages 00–00 as a guide, cut the 4½"-wide strips into segments ranging from 3" to 20" in length, cutting the ends of the segments at 45° angles parallel to each other. Note the direction of the 45° angles on the strips. Use the pieced fabric illustrations as a guide for the length and number of segments to cut from each fabric, as well as their placement in the jacket. For the front pockets, cut one 11" segment from fabric A, one 8¾" segment from fabric B, and one 3" segment from fabric C, taking care to cut the segments so the ends angle in the proper direction. (Refer to the illustrations on page 11.) For the sleeves, cut four segments about 30" long. The segments should be slightly longer than the sleeves, not including the pointed ends of the segments. Set the pocket segments and four sleeve segments aside.

sweatshirt preparation

Read the "General Instructions" on page 5 before starting your project.

1. Follow the steps for "Deconstructing the Sweatshirt" on page 5, creating side seams for this jacket as instructed in step 2. In step 4, cut off the shoulder seam allowances on the seam line along the shoulder seams, cutting straight through the neckband. *Do not* cut the neckband off.

2. Follow the steps for "Interfacing and Prepping the Sweatshirt" on page 6, except in step 1, draw a vertical line at the center front on the *wrong* side of the sweatshirt. No new neckline markings are needed. The existing neckline will be used. Continue as in step 3 on page 6.

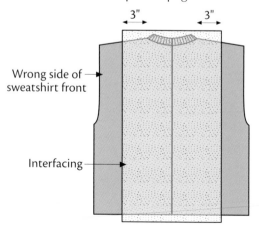

Mark the sweatshirt, apply interfacing, and cut on the marked line.

jacket front and back

This project uses ¼"-wide seam allowances unless otherwise noted.

1. Using the pieced fabric illustrations below and on page 11 as a guide, sew 4½"-wide segments together to make 12 strips long enough to cover the sweatshirt front and back pieces, not including the pointed ends of the segments (about 37" to 42" long, depending on the sweatshirt size). Press the seam allowances in one direction. Trim off points.

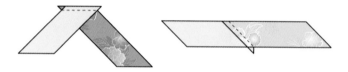

2. Using the illustration as a guide, lay out the six pieced strips for the jacket back. Note the direction of the diagonal seams on each strip. Join the strips, starting at the center back and working toward the sides. Press the seam allowances open. The fabric should be wide enough to cover the sweatshirt back. If it isn't, add another row of pieced segments to each side of the pieced fabric.

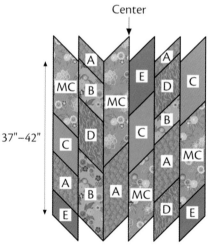

Pieced fabric for jacket back

3. Lay the sweatshirt back on a cutting table, wrong side up. Cover the sweatshirt back with the pieced fabric, aligning the center of the fabric with the center back of the sweatshirt. Pin the layers together with safety pins. Quilt by stitching in the ditch on all seam lines using a walking foot.

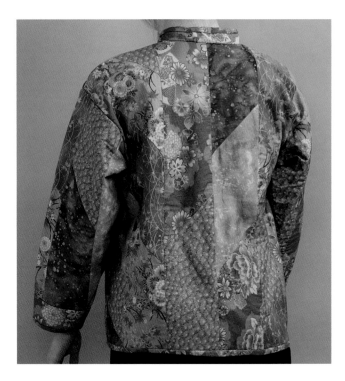

4. Machine baste ¼" from the edges of the sweatshirt back and stay stitch around the back neckline ¼" below the neckband. Trim away the excess fabric. Cut off and discard the sweatshirt neckband.

5. Sew the 3" pocket segment to the 8¾" pocket segment as shown for the left pocket.

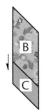

Left pocket

6. Fold a 2" x 8" bias strip in half, wrong sides together. Pin the strip to the upper edge of a pocket and stitch ¼" from the edges. Fold the binding to the back so the fold line just covers the machine stitching. Hand stitch in place. Trim the edges even. Repeat with the 11" pocket segment.

7. Using the pieced fabric illustrations above right as a guide, lay out the pieced strips for the left front and the right front, noting the direction of the diagonal seams. Pin the pocket front pieces to the corresponding center strips of the left and right fronts and baste the pocket pieces to the strips ⅛" from the side edges.

8. Realign the left front strips and sew them together. Press the seam allowances open. The fabric should be wide enough to cover the left front sweatshirt. If it isn't, add another row of pieced segments to the side of the pieced fabric that will be at the side seam. Repeat with the right front strips.

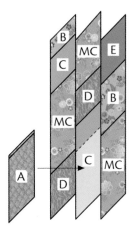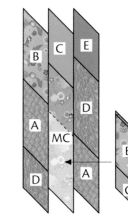

Pocket   Pieced fabric   Pieced fabric   Pocket
        for right front   for left front

9. Lay the sweatshirt left front piece on a cutting table, wrong side up. Position the pieced fabric for the left front, right side up, over the sweatshirt, aligning the center front edges. Pin the layers together with safety pins. Stitch in the ditch on all the seam lines using a walking foot. Mark a diagonal line 6¼" down and parallel to the upper edge of the pocket using a fabric pen. Stitch on the marked line. Repeat for the right front piece.

10. Machine baste ¼" from the edges of the sweatshirt front pieces and stay stitch around the front neckline ¼" below the neckband. Trim away the excess pieced fabric. Cut off and discard the sweatshirt neckband pieces.

sleeves

1. Using the pieced fabric illustrations for the sleeves on page 12 as a guide, sew 4½"-wide segments together to make six center strips about 30" long (or as long as the sweatshirt sleeves, without including the pointed ends of the segments). Note the direction of the diagonal seams. Press the seam allowances in one direction.

2. Lay out the three pieced strips for the center section of each sleeve. Join the strips. Sew a 30" unpieced strip to each side of the pieced section. Press the seam allowances open. The pieced fabrics should be wide enough to cover the sweatshirt sleeves. If they aren't, stitch another segment to each side of the pieced fabric as needed.

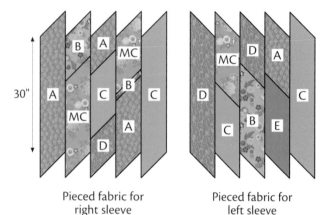

Pieced fabric for right sleeve

Pieced fabric for left sleeve

3. Lay the sweatshirt sleeves on a cutting table, wrong side up. Cover the left sweatshirt sleeve with the corresponding pieced fabric. Align the center of the fabric with the center of the sleeve and pin the layers together with safety pins. Stitch in the ditch on all seam lines using a walking foot. Repeat for the right sleeve.

4. Machine baste ¼" from the edges of the sweatshirt sleeves and trim away the excess pieced fabric.

cuffs

1. Measure the sleeve width 2½" up from the lower edge. Cut two 5"-wide cuffs from turquoise floral to the determined measurement. Fold each cuff piece wrong sides together and press. Cut a rectangle of interfacing to cover half of each cuff. Trim ¼" from one long edge. Open the cuff and fuse the interfacing in place as shown, following the manufacturer's instructions. Fold the cuff in half again and press.

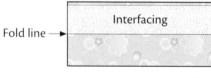

Apply interfacing to cuff.

2. Center and pin the long raw edges of one cuff to the lower edge of a sleeve, right sides together, and stitch a scant ¼" from the edge. Repeat for the remaining cuff. Trim the side edges of the cuffs even with the side edges of the sleeves and baste the edges together at the sides.

shoulder seams

1. Pin the jacket front pieces to the jacket back at the shoulder seams, aligning the edges at the neck and armhole. If the shoulder widths are off a bit, align the edges at the armhole. The neckline edges can be trimmed up later for a smooth transition.

2. Stitch shoulders; press the seam allowances open. If the shoulder widths did not align at the neckline, trim them now.

mandarin collar

1. Measure the neck opening, ¼" in from the edge. From the turquoise floral fabric, cut a 3"-wide strip to the determined length.

2. Cut a piece of interfacing ¼" smaller than the collar piece all around and fuse the interfacing to the wrong side of the collar following the manufacturer's instructions.

3. Fold the collar in half, wrong sides together, and press. Using the computer CD as a template, mark rounded upper corners on both ends, leaving the lower ¼" straight at each side of the collar. Cut on the marked lines. Press ¼" to the wrong side on one long edge of the collar.

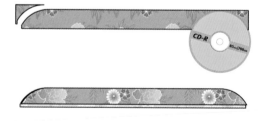

4. Open the collar, fold in half crosswise, and pin-mark the center of each long edge. Pin the long unpressed edge of the collar to the jacket neckline, right sides together, matching the center pin mark to the center back seam and matching the ends. Clip to the stay stitching if necessary. Sew the collar to the jacket. Press the seam allowance toward the collar and grade the seam allowances. (Grading is the trimming of seam allowances to different widths, with the seam allowance that will fall nearest the garment side cut the narrowest. The result is a seam that lies flat without causing a bulky ridge.) Fold the collar in half, wrong sides together, and pin the pressed edge of the collar over the seam line. Hand stitch in place. The remaining collar edges will be covered with binding later.

jacket assembly and finishing

1. Refer to the instructions for "Binding" on page 6 to make the jacket binding. Sew a strip of binding to the lower edge of each sleeve; press away from the shoulder. Do not fold over or finish off.

2. Pin the sleeves, right sides together, to the jacket front and back around the armholes, aligning the pin marks on the sleeves with the shoulder seams. Ease as necessary. Be sure to pin the left sleeve to the left side of the jacket and the right sleeve to the right side of the jacket. Stitch around the armhole using ½"-wide seam allowances. Press the seam allowances toward the sleeves.

3. Pin the long edges of each sleeve right sides together. Pin the jacket front to the back, right sides together along the side seams, matching the armhole seams. Stitch the arm seam from the cuff to the armhole and stitch the side seams from the bottom edge to the armhole using ½"-wide seam allowances. Press the seam allowances open.

4. Turn the binding on the sleeve to the wrong side so it just covers the stitching line and hand stitch in place. Turn the jacket right side out.

5. Bind the remaining edges of the jacket, starting at the lower edge of the jacket back.

6. Cut three 1" x 20" strips from the turquoise floral fabric for the button loops. Fold each strip, right sides together, and stitch ¼" from the long raw edges. Turn right side out using a bodkin or safety pin. Cut off a 5"-long segment from one of the strips. Tie three knots approximately in the middle of the segment. Place the two ends into the hole of a replica Chinese coin. Poke a ¼" hole through the left front jacket, about 1" down from the collar seam and about 1½" in from the outer edge of the center front binding, with the sharp point of a pair of scissors. With a blunt instrument insert the two tails on the back of the coin to the wrong side of the jacket and hand stitch in place. Repeat this process to attach two more coins on the same side of the jacket, spacing the coins about 4½" apart down the front of the jacket.

7. With the remaining 15" tube segment, tie three knots approximately 4" from one end. Insert the two ends into a coin as before, but this time the long end will make a loop. Poke a ¼" hole through the right front of the jacket, about 1" down from the collar seam and about 1½" in from the edge of the center front binding across from the button on the left front. With a blunt instrument insert the two ends of the tube on the back of the coin to the wrong side of the jacket. Carefully pull the loop across the jacket and loop around the coin on the left side to check the fit. Adjust the loop size as necessary by pulling on the loop itself or by pulling on the tail of the loop on the inside of the jacket. Pin the end of the loop in place when the perfect length is achieved, unbutton the loop, and hand stitch the tails in place, trimming any excess. Repeat this process to attach two more coins with loops on the same side of the jacket, spacing the coins about 4½" apart.

Insert ends into hole in jacket.

Elaborate front closures, consisting of fabric tube loops, replica Chinese coins, and fabric knots, are reminiscent of a Chinese jacket with all the appropriate details.

spring trees

Light and medium colors are combined in the body of this jacket. A dark fabric used for sashing, binding, and sleeve bands accents and frames the jacket. The asymmetrical front features a single loop-and-button closure.

materials

Fabric quantities are listed by the size of the sweatshirt. Purchase a sweatshirt one size larger than you'd normally wear. For example, a size Medium sweatshirt becomes a size Small jacket. This jacket was designed to have the right front overlap the left by a couple of inches rather than have the front edges just meet. This removes some of the wearing ease, which allows the jacket to fit more like a jacket rather than fit loose like a sweatshirt. Note: This was a fabric group—all the same print, but in different colors.

	Medium	Large	XL	2XL	3XL
Green print	1¾ yards	1¾ yards	2 yards	2 yards	2 yards
Tan print	⅜ yard	⅜ yard	⅝ yard	⅝ yard	⅝ yard
Light brown print	⅜ yard	⅜ yard	⅝ yard	⅝ yard	⅝ yard
Taupe print	⅜ yard	⅜ yard	½ yard	½ yard	½ yard
Brown print	1 yard	1 yard	1⅛ yards	1⅛ yards	1⅛ yards
Medium-weight fusible interfacing	¾ yard	¾ yard	⅞ yard	⅞ yard	⅞ yard
Additional supplies	Sweatshirt Other supplies listed on page 5 1 button, at least 1¼" in diameter				

cutting
(for sizes medium and large)

From the brown print, cut:

6 strips, 1½" x 42"

2" bias strips (enough to go around the edges of the jacket plus 20" for the button loop, mitered corners, and finishing—about 125" to 140"). See "Binding" on page 6 for instructions on cutting the strips.

From the green print *and* the taupe print, cut:

2 strips (3 strips for size Large), 3" x 42"; crosscut into squares, 3" x 3", to yield enough for your size

From the tan print *and* the light brown print, cut:

3 strips, 3" x 42"; crosscut into squares, 3" x 3", to yield enough for your size

cutting
(for sizes XL, 2XL, and 3XL)

From the brown print, cut:

6 strips, 1½" x 42"

2" bias strips (enough to go around the edges of the jacket plus 20" for the button loop, mitered corners and finishing—about 135" to 150"). See "Binding" on page 6 for instructions on cutting the strips.

From the green print *and* the taupe print, cut:

3 strips, 3½" x 42"; crosscut into squares, 3½" x 3½", to yield enough for your size

From the tan print *and* the light brown print, cut:

4 strips, 3½" x 42"; crosscut into squares, 3½" x 3½", to yield enough for your size

sweatshirt preparation

Read the "General Instructions" on page 5 before starting your project.

1. Follow the steps for "Deconstructing the Sweatshirt" on page 5. After removing the band at the bottom of the sweatshirt in step 1, measure 3" up from the lower edge and draw a new horizontal hemline. Cut along the marked line through both layers. Create side seams as instructed in step 2. In step 4, cut off the shoulder seam allowances on the seam line, cutting straight through the neckband. *Do not* cut off the neckband.

2. Follow the steps for "Interfacing and Prepping the Sweatshirt" on page 6. In step 1, on the right side of the sweatshirt, mark the front opening by drawing a vertical line on the left front of the sweatshirt, straight down from the outermost edge of the neckline to the lower edge. Measure up from the lower edge along the marked line the number of inches indicated for your size and mark a dot. On the right front of the sweatshirt, draw a diagonal line from the outermost edge of the neck opening to the marked dot on the left. Continue as in step 3 on page 6.

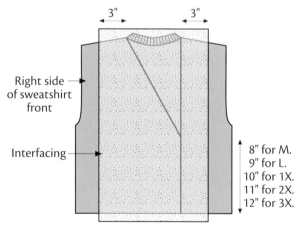

Right side of sweatshirt front

Interfacing

8" for M.
9" for L.
10" for 1X.
11" for 2X.
12" for 3X.

Mark the sweatshirt, apply interfacing, and cut on the marked lines.

jacket back

This project uses ¼"-wide seam allowances unless otherwise noted.

1. Sew squares together in random order to make pieced strips as illustrated below. Press the seam allowances to one side. Join the strips to make pieced units as shown. Press the seam allowances to one side. (Be sure the pieced units will be large enough to cover the sweatshirt back after joining them together with brown strips. To make the fabric larger than what is shown, add more squares to the bottom and sides only, extending the brown strips as needed.) Join the units with 1½"-wide brown strips as shown. Press the seam allowances toward the brown strips. The pieced fabric should be large enough to cover the sweatshirt back, with the centerline of the fabric placed on the centerline of the sweatshirt.

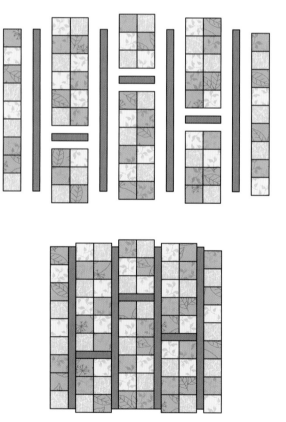

Pieced fabric for jacket back

2. Lay the sweatshirt back on a cutting table, right side up. Cover the sweatshirt back with the pieced fabric, aligning the centers. Pin the layers together with safety pins. Quilt as desired with free-motion quilting; do not quilt the brown strips.

3. Machine baste ¼" from the edges of the sweatshirt back and stay stitch around the back neckline ¼" below the neckband. Trim away the excess pieced fabric. Cut off and discard the sweatshirt neckband.

left front

1. In the same manner as for the back, sew squares together in random order to make pieced units as illustrated. Join the units with 1½"-wide brown strips as shown. The pieced fabric should be large enough to cover the left sweatshirt front. To make the fabric larger than what is shown, add more squares to the bottom and left side only, extending the brown strips as needed.

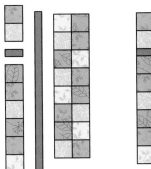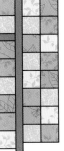

Pieced fabric
for left front

2. Lay the left front sweatshirt on a cutting table, right side up. Cover the sweatshirt with the pieced fabric. Take care to place the fabric on the sweatshirt so the horizontal seams at the side seams will align with the horizontal seams of the jacket back piece. Pin the layers together and quilt as for the jacket back.

3. Machine baste ¼" from the edges of the left front sweatshirt and trim away the excess pieced fabric.

right front

1. Cut a rectangle of green print fabric at least 1" larger all around than the right front sweatshirt. Measure the left front from the left side edge to the center of the 1" brown strip. For the remainder of this step, the terms *left* and *right* refer to the unit as shown in the illustration, not the unit as worn on the body. Mark this same distance, plus 1" extra, from the left edge of the green rectangle. Draw a vertical line through the rectangle at this point. Cut along the marked line. Join the two fabric pieces back together with a 1½"-wide brown strip between them. Press the seam allowances toward the brown strip.

Pieced fabric for right front
(as worn on the body)

2. Lay the right front sweatshirt on a cutting table, right side up, and lay the pieced fabric right side up over it, taking care to place the brown strip at the shoulder the same distance from the armhole edge as the brown strip in the left front piece. Pin the layers together with safety pins and quilt as desired; do not quilt the brown strips.

3. Machine baste ¼" from the edges of the right front sweatshirt and trim away the excess fabric.

sleeves

1. To accommodate the 2¼" contrasting sleeve band, trim 2" or the desired amount from the lower edge of the sweatshirt sleeves, depending on the length of the sleeves after removing the original sweatshirt sleeve band. Using the sweatshirt sleeve as a pattern, cut two pieces of green print slightly larger than the sweatshirt sleeves and place the pieces right sides together. Draw a vertical centerline on the top sleeve with chalk or a fabric pen. Draw in the horizontal lines as shown below. Cut on the marked lines through both layers of fabric.

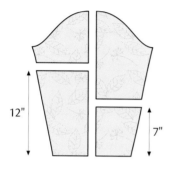

2. Carefully move the top fabric layers to the side and keep in the same order. The piecing arrangement for the left sleeve is the mirror image of the right sleeve. Work on one sleeve at a time to avoid confusion. Join the top units to the bottom units with a 1½"-wide brown strip between them; press toward the brown strips. Join the two vertical halves with a 1½"-wide brown strip between them; press toward the brown strip. Repeat for the remaining sleeve, making it the mirror image of the first sleeve.

3. Lay the sweatshirt sleeves on a cutting table, right side up. Cover the sweatshirt sleeves with the corresponding pieced sleeves, aligning the center-lines. Pin the layers together with safety pins and quilt as desired; do not quilt the brown strips.

4. Machine baste ¼" from the edges of the sweatshirt sleeves and trim away the excess fabric.

sleeve band

1. Measure the sleeve width ¼" up from the lower edge. Cut two 5"-wide bands to the determined measurement.

2. Fold each band piece wrong sides together and press. Cut a rectangle of interfacing to cover half of each band and trim away ¼" from one long edge. Open each band and fuse the interfacing in place as shown, following the manufacturer's instructions. Press ¼" to the wrong side on the long edge of the sleeve band that is without interfacing. Refold the band.

Apply interfacing to band.

3. Pin the long edge of the band on the interfaced side to the lower edge of the sleeve, right sides together. Stitch ¼" from the edges. Press the seam allowances toward the band. Refold the band and place the sleeve on a cutting mat. Align a ruler with a long edge of the sleeve and trim any excess from the side edge of the band. Repeat on the other side. Attach the band to the second sleeve in the same manner. The band will be completed in later steps.

jacket assembly

1. Pin the jacket front pieces to the jacket back at the shoulder seams, aligning the edges at the neck and armhole. If the shoulder widths are off a bit, align the edges at the armhole. The neckline edges can be trimmed later for a smooth transition.

2. Using ½"-wide seam allowances, stitch the shoulders. Press the seam allowances toward the back and topstitch ¼" from the seam line. If the shoulder widths did not align at the neckline, trim them now.

3. Pin the sleeves, right sides together, to the jacket front and back around the armholes, aligning the pin marks on the sleeves with the shoulder seams. Ease as necessary. Be sure to pin the left sleeve to the left side of the jacket and the right sleeve to the right side of the jacket. Stitch around the armhole using a ¼" seam allowance. Press the seam allowances toward the sleeves.

4. Pin the jacket front to the back along the side seams and long sleeve edges, matching the seams at the underarm and sleeve bands. Stitch from the lower edge of the opened sleeve band to the underarm seam and stitch the side seam from the lower edge to the underarm seam using ¼" seam allowances. Press the seam allowances to one side.

5. Fold the sleeve band to the wrong side on the pressed line and hand stitch in place, just covering the seam line. Turn the jacket right side out.

6. Bind the edges of the jacket starting on the right front at the point where the neckline begins, binding the front edge first, and then the lower edge, following the instructions for "Binding" on page 6. When the starting point is reached, backstitch and leave at least 10" of extra binding to create a button loop. Trim off the remainder.

button loop

1. Press ¼" to the wrong side on the long edges of the extra binding. Fold in half lengthwise and stitch the long edges together by hand. Fold the binding in half and shape the end as shown below to create the button loop. Check the size of the loop against the button and adjust the length as necessary. Stitch the end of the loop to the wrong side of the jacket. Hand stitch across the edge of the triangle formed at the end of the button loop as shown.

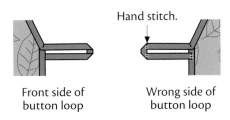

Front side of button loop   Wrong side of button loop

2. Sew the button on the left front across from the button loop.

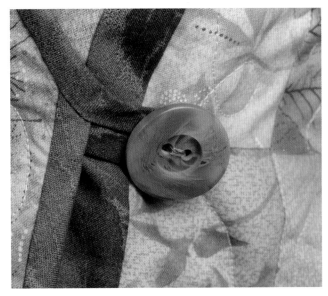

An oversized button adds designer detail to the jacket. The front bias binding transitions seamlessly into a button loop.

pure and simple black and white

Rounded corners, highlighted with contrasting binding, add couture detailing to a simple jacket. Pieced squares, set on point, add visual interest to the jacket with subtle pattern changes. Piecing also highlights the lower edges of the sleeves.

materials

Fabric quantities are listed by the size of the sweatshirt. Purchase the sweatshirt size you'd normally wear.

	Small	Medium	Large	XL	2XL	3XL
Leaf print	2 yards	2 yards	2½ yards	2½ yards	3 yards	3⅛ yards
Floral print	½ yard	½ yard	⅝ yard	⅝ yard	¾ yard	¾ yard
Toile	½ yard	½ yard	⅝ yard	⅝ yard	¾ yard	¾ yard
Black solid	¾ yard	¾ yard	¾ yard	¾ yard	1 yard	1 yard
Medium-weight fusible interfacing	¾ yard	¾ yard	¾ yard	¾ yard	⅞ yard	⅞ yard
Additional supplies	Sweatshirt Other supplies listed on page 5 2 buttons, at least 2" in diameter Computer CD for template					

cutting
(for sizes small, medium, and large)

From the leaf print, cut:

4 strips (or more, depending on the sweatshirt size), 3" x 42"; crosscut into squares, 3" x 3", to yield enough for your size

From the floral print *and* the toile, cut:

3 strips (or more, depending on the sweatshirt size), 3" x 42"; crosscut into squares, 3" x 3", to yield enough for your size

From the black solid, cut:

2"-wide bias strips (enough to go around jacket and sleeves, plus 25" for button loops, mitered corners, and finishing—about 215" to 235"). See "Binding" on page 6.

cutting
(for sizes XL, 2XL, and 3XL)

From the leaf print, cut:

4 strips (or more, depending on the sweatshirt size), 4" x 42"; crosscut into squares, 4" x 4", to yield enough for your size

From the floral print *and* the toile, cut:

4 strips (or more, depending on the sweatshirt size), 4" x 42"; crosscut into squares, 4" x 4", to yield enough for your size

From the black fabric, cut:

2"-wide bias strips (enough to go around jacket and sleeves, plus 25" for button loops, mitered corners and finishing—about 225" to 245"). See "Binding" on page 6.

sweatshirt preparation

Read the "General Instructions" on page 5 before starting your project.

1. Follow the steps for "Deconstructing the Sweatshirt" on page 5. After removing the band at the bottom of the sweatshirt in step 1, measure 2" or the desired amount up from the lower edge and draw a new horizontal hemline. Cut on the marked line through both layers. Create side seams for this jacket as instructed in step 2. In step 4, cut off the shoulder seam allowances on the seam line, cutting straight through the neckband. *Do not cut off the neckband.*

2. Follow the steps for "Interfacing and Prepping the Sweatshirt" on page 6. In step 1, on the right side of the sweatshirt, mark the front opening by drawing a vertical line on the front left of the sweatshirt straight down from outermost edge of the left neckline to the lower edge. Draw the neck opening as shown below using the measurements given for your size. Trace around a CD to mark the rounded corners for the jacket right front as indicated. Continue as in step 3 on page 6.

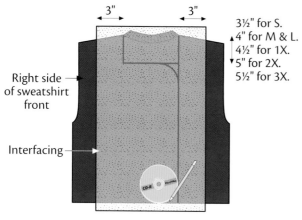

Right side of sweatshirt front

Interfacing

3"   3"

3½" for S.
4" for M & L.
4½" for 1X.
5" for 2X.
5½" for 3X.

Mark the sweatshirt, apply interfacing, and cut on the marked lines.

jacket back

This project uses ¼"-wide seam allowances unless otherwise noted.

1. Sew squares together in random order to make strips. Join the strips to create pieced fabric large enough to cover the sweatshirt back when the squares are placed on point.

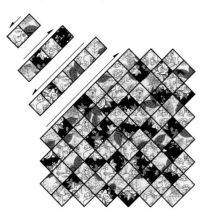

Pieced fabric for jacket back

2. Lay the sweatshirt back on a cutting table, right side up. Cover the sweatshirt back with the pieced fabric so the squares are on point. Align the centerline of the fabric with the center back of the sweatshirt and pin the layers together with safety pins. Quilt by stitching in the ditch on all seam lines using a walking foot.

3. Machine baste ¼" from the edges of the sweatshirt back and stay stitch around the back neckline ¼" below the neckband. Trim away the excess pieced fabric. Cut off and discard the sweatshirt neckband.

4. Trace around a computer CD to mark the rounded corners for the lower edges of the jacket back. Trim on the marked lines.

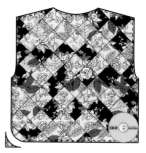

left front

1. Make pieced fabric to cover the left front sweatshirt in the same manner as for the sweatshirt back.

2. Lay the left front sweatshirt on a cutting table, right side up. Cover the sweatshirt with the pieced fabric so the squares in the fabric are on point. Take care to place the fabric on the sweatshirt so the pieced seams at the side seam will align with the pieced seams at the side seam of the jacket back. Pin the layers together with safety pins. Quilt as for the jacket back.

3. Machine baste ¼" from the edges of the sweatshirt and trim away the excess pieced fabric. Trace around a computer CD to mark the rounded corners at the lower edges as shown. Trim on the marked lines.

right front

1. Cut a rectangle out of leaf print fabric, slightly larger than the right front sweatshirt. Lay the right front sweatshirt on a cutting table, right side up, with the fabric right side up on top. Pin the layers

together with safety pins. Quilt as desired using free-motion quilting.

2. Machine baste ¼" from the edges of the right front sweatshirt and trim away the excess fabric. Trace around a computer CD to mark the rounded corner at the lower right edge as shown. Trim on the marked line.

sleeves

1. Fold a piece of leaf print fabric, wrong sides together, and lay a sweatshirt sleeve on top. Trace around the sleeve with a fabric pen, and then remove the sleeve. Redraw the lower edge of the sleeve 3" above the marked line for sizes Small, Medium, or Large, or 4" above the marked line for sizes XL, 2XL, or 3XL. Cut out the sleeves.

2. Sew squares together in random order to make a strip at least as long as the width across the lower edge of each sleeve. Center and pin a pieced strip of squares to the lower edge of each sleeve, right sides together. Stitch ¼" from the raw edges. Press the seam allowances toward the pieced strips.

3. Lay the sweatshirt sleeves on a cutting table, right sides up. Cover the sleeves with the corresponding fabric sleeve, aligning the lower edges as close as possible. Pin the layers together with safety pins and quilt as for the right front jacket piece.

4. Machine baste ¼" from the edges of the sweatshirt sleeves. Trim away any excess fabric. Trace around a computer CD to mark the rounded corners for the lower edges of the sleeves. Cut on the marked lines.

jacket assembly

1. Pin the jacket front pieces to the jacket back at the shoulder seams, aligning the edges at the neck and armhole. If the shoulder widths are off a bit, align the edges at the armhole. The neckline edges can be trimmed up later for a smooth transition.

2. Stitch the shoulders using ¼" seam allowances. Press the seam allowances to the back. If the shoulder seams did not align at the neckline, trim them now.

3. Pin the sleeves, right sides together, to the jacket front and back around the armholes, aligning the pin marks on the sleeves with the shoulder seams. Be sure to pin the left sleeve to the left side of the jacket and the right sleeve to the right side of the jacket. Stitch around the armhole using ¼" seam allowances. Press the seam allowances toward the sleeves. *Do not* sew side seams or sleeve seams.

finishing

1. Refer to the instructions for "Binding" on page 6. Bind the edges of the sleeves, starting 5" above the lower edge on one side and ending 5" above the lower edge on the oppsite side, taking care to ease the binding around the corners. Bind the jacket front and neck areas starting at the left side seam 5" above the lower edge. Sew binding along the bottom edge, up the front, around the neck, down the right front, across the bottom, and up the right side seam to 5" above the lower edge. Bind the lower edge of the jacket back in the same manner.

2. Pin the jacket right sides together along the side seams and sleeve seams. Stitch the side seams using ¼" seam allowances, starting ½" below where the binding begins and ending at the armhole seam, catching the ends of the binding in the seams. Stitch the sleeve seams, starting ½" below where the binding begins and ending at the armhole. Hand stitch the ends of the binding to the inside of the jacket. Turn the jacket right side out. If desired, turn up a cuff on the lower edge of the sleeves.

button loops

From the leftover binding strip, cut a 1⅛" x 15" strip and fold in half lengthwise, right sides together. Sew ¼" from the long raw edges. Turn inside out with a bodkin or safety pin. Make a loop big enough to accommodate the button plus ½" extra at both ends. Trim off the excess. Determine the placement of the loop at the top of the right front jacket just inside the binding and pin in place on the wrong side. Hand stitch the loop in place. Make a second loop and secure to the jacket 8½" down from the first loop. Sew the buttons on the left front across from the button loops.

pickin'
daisies

Front and back yokes with stitched tucks accent a boxy jacket. Plaid bias trim highlights the edges and is used for matching sleeve bands. The jacket closes at the center front with three buttons and simple button loops.

materials					
Fabric quantities are listed by the size of the sweatshirt. Purchase the sweatshirt size you'd normally wear. This jacket has long sleeves. Refer to "Choosing a Sweatshirt" on page 5 for guidance in selecting the appropriate size and sleeve length.					
	Small	**Medium**	**Large**	**XL**	**2XL**	**3XL**
Large-scale floral	1¾ yards	1¾ yards	2 yards	3 yards	3⅛ yards	3¼ yards
Light green floral	¼ yard	¼ yard	¼ yard	¼ yard	¼ yard	¼ yard
Olive print	¼ yard	¼ yard	¼ yard	¼ yard	¼ yard	¼ yard
Pink floral	¼ yard	¼ yard	¼ yard	¼ yard	¼ yard	¼ yard
Ivory dotted fabric	¼ yard	¼ yard	¼ yard	¼yard	¼ yard	¼ yard
Plaid	1 yard	1 yard	1 yard	1 yard	1 yard	1 yard
Medium-weight fusible interfacing	¾ yard	⅞ yard	⅞ yard	1 yard	1 yard	1 yard
Additional supplies	Sweatshirt Other supplies listed on page 5 3 buttons, at least 1½" in diameter					

cutting

From the plaid, cut:

3"-wide bias strips (enough to go around the edges of the jacket, plus 10" for mitered corners and finishing, plus 24" for button loops—about 180" to 210"). See "Binding" on page 6 for instructions on cutting the strips.

From all remaining fabrics, cut:

3 strips, 2" x 42"

sweatshirt preparation

Read the "General Instructions" on page 5 before starting your project.

1. Follow the steps for "Deconstructing the Sweatshirt" on page 5. After removing the band from the bottom of the sweatshirt in step 1, measure 1" up from the lower edge and draw a new horizontal hemline. Cut along the marked line through both layers. Do not cut the side seams. In step 4, draw a new shoulder seam on each side that tapers from the neckband to ½" lower than the existing shoulder seam at the armhole edge. Cut along the marked lines through both layers, cutting straight through the neckband. *Do not* cut the neckband off.

2. Follow the steps for "Interfacing and Prepping the Sweatshirt" on page 6. In step 1, draw a vertical line at the center front on the right side of the sweatshirt. The existing neckline will be used and no new markings are needed. Continue as in steps

2 and 3. In step 3 be sure to cut through the front layer of the sweatshirt only.

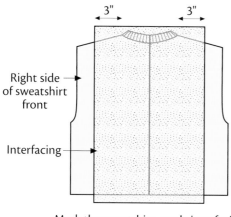

Mark the sweatshirt, apply interfacing, and cut on the marked line.

quilting the front and back

1. Lay the sweatshirt on a flat surface, right side up. Cut a piece of large-scale floral on the crosswise grain of the fabric to cover the sweatshirt from the lower edge to 3" above the armhole openings.

2. Cover the sweatshirt with the fabric, placing the grain line of the fabric perpendicular to the lower edge; pin the layers together with safety pins. Quilt over the floral fabric as desired, starting at the back.

3. Machine baste ¼" from the edges of the sweatshirt where it's covered with fabric. Trim away the excess fabric.

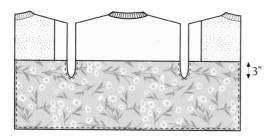

back and front tucks

1. Measure from the shoulder at the armhole edge down the back, the amount shown for your size in the illustration at step 6. Draw a horizontal placement line with chalk or a fabric pen, to mark the first tuck. You should be drawing on the quilted fabric. Adjust placement if necessary.

2. Fold a 2" fabric strip in half lengthwise; press. Place the strip on the sweatshirt back with the raw edges on the marked line. Sew ¼" from the raw edges, stretching the fabric slightly. Trim off the excess strip and reserve it for later use. Repeat with another strip of a different color, only this time place the folded edge of the strip so it just covers the sewing line of the previous strip.

3. Refering to the photo on page 24 and the illustration after step 6, continue adding strips in the same manner until the upper portion of the back is covered with strips. Machine baste ¼" from the edges of the sweatshirt (where it is covered by tucks) and stay stitch ¼" below the neckband. Trim away any excess fabric.

4. Add strips to the sweatshirt front sections in the same manner and in the same order as for the sweatshirt back.

5. Find the center back of the jacket. Measure 1" to each side of the center and draw vertical lines on the tucks with chalk. Measure out 2" from the marked lines and draw two more lines. Continue in this manner until you are within 2" of the armhole edge.

6. Stitch on the marked lines to keep the tucks flat, starting at the shoulder or neckline and backstitching at the end of the last tuck.

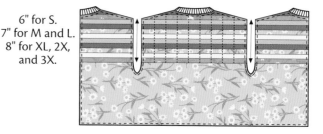

6" for S.
7" for M and L.
8" for XL, 2X, and 3X.

7. Starting at the armhole, draw vertical lines 2" apart over the tucks of the front jacket sections, aligning them with the stitched lines of the back at the shoulder. Sew the tucks down in the same manner as for the back.

8. Cut off and discard the front and back neckbands.

shoulder seams

1. Pin the jacket fronts to the jacket back at the shoulder seams, aligning the edges at the neck and armhole, and aligning the stitched tuck lines. If the

shoulder widths are off a bit, align the edges at the armhole. The neckline edges can be trimmed later for a smooth transition.

2. Stitch the shoulders using ½" seam allowances. Press the seam allowances open. Grade the seam allowances if necessary to reduce bulk. (Grading is the trimming of seam allowances to different widths, with the seam allowance that will fall nearest the garment side cut the narrowest.) If the shoulder widths did not align at the neckline, trim them now.

sleeves

1. From the remaining large-scale floral, cut fabric to cover the two sleeves, cutting on the crosswise grain to match the direction of the pattern on the jacket. Lay the sweatshirt sleeves on a cutting table, right side up. Cover the sleeves with fabric, aligning the grain line of the fabric with the sleeve center. Pin the layers together with safety pins and quilt in the same manner as for the jacket.

2. Machine baste ¼" from the edges of the sweatshirt sleeves and trim away the excess fabric.

sleeve band

1. Measure the width of the sleeve 2¼" above the lower edge. Cut two 2½" strips from plaid fabric to the determined measurement. Press ¼" to the right side on both long sides of each band.

2. Open out the pressed seam allowance on one side of the band and pin the right side of this edge to the *wrong* side of the sweatshirt sleeve at the lower edge. Stitch along the pressed crease line. Press the seam allowances toward the sweatshirt and grade the seam allowances if necessary. Fold the band over the sleeve; press. Stitch the band ¼" from the lower edge on the right side; press.

3. Pin the band to the sleeve at the folded upper edge and stitch ⅛" from the edge. Trim the side edges of the band even with the edges of the sleeve. Stitch the band to the remaining sleeve in the same manner.

finishing

1. Pin the long edges of each sleeve right sides together and stitch using a ½" seam allowance. Press the seam allowances open. Machine tack the seam allowances open at the lower edge of the sleeves. Turn the sleeves right sides out.

2. Pin the sleeves, right sides together, to the jacket around the armholes, matching the pin marks on the sleeves to the shoulder seams and easing as necessary. Be sure to pin the left sleeve to the left side of the jacket and the right sleeve to the right side of the jacket.

3. Stitch around the armhole using ½" seam allowances. Press toward the sleeves.

4. Refer to the instructions for "Binding" on page 6 and bind the edges of the jacket, starting at the lower edge of the jacket back.

5. Cut a 1½" x 24" bias strip from the remainder of the bias binding. Fold, right sides together, and stitch ¼" from the raw edges. Turn right side out with a bodkin or safety pin. Press the tube. Fold the tube in half and stitch close to the folded edges to create a strip for the button loops.

6. Stitch three buttons to the left side of the jacket front just inside the binding, placing the second button at the point where the tucks end and placing the third button the same distance apart as the first two.

7. Determine what size loop is needed to go around the buttons when the loop ends are stitched to the back of the right jacket front, just inside the binding. Cut the bias strips to the determined length and machine stitch the ends in place so the loops line up with the buttons on the left side of the jacket.

The narrow loop closure nicely complements the jacket without detracting from the tucks and bias detailing.

tucks on the diagonal

Subtle pleat detailing on the front, back, and sleeve bands adds textural interest to a short jacket with ¾-length sleeves. The asymmetrical front opening with button-and-loop closures gives it a couture finish.

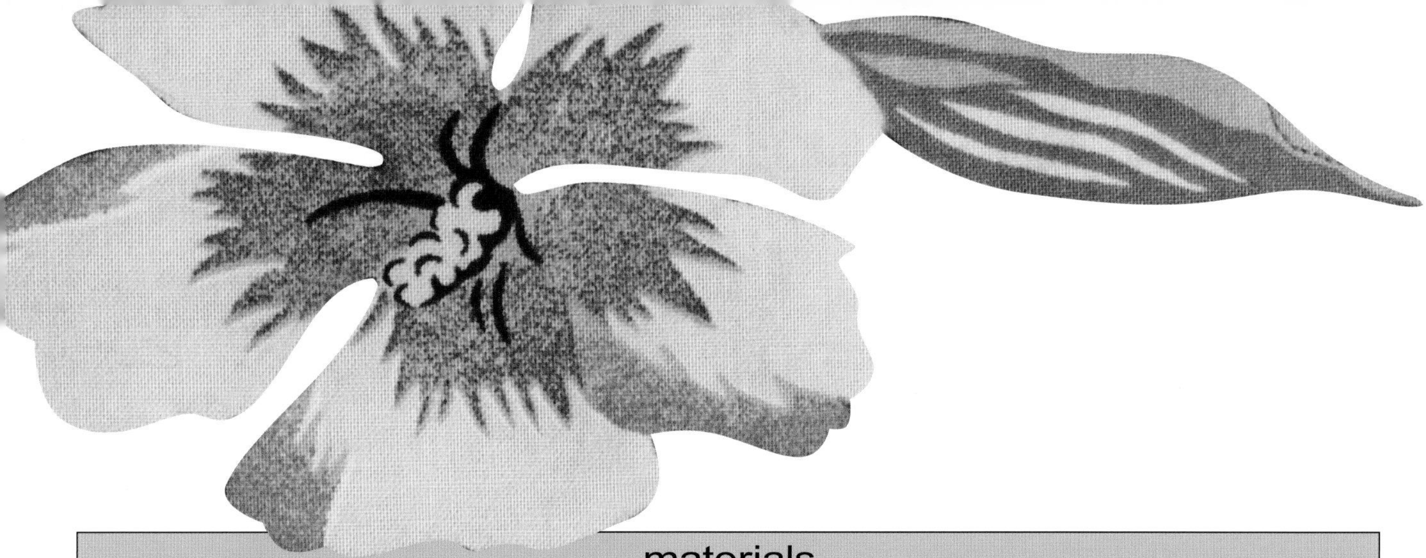

materials

Fabric quantities are listed by the size of the sweatshirt. Purchase the sweatshirt size you'd normally wear.

	Small	Medium	Large	XL	2XL	3XL
Large-scale floral	3 yards	3⅛ yards	3⅛ yards	3¼ yards	3⅜ yards	4⅜ yards
Green floral	½ yard	½ yard	½ yard	½ yard	⅝ yard	⅝ yard
Blue print	¼ yard	¼ yard	¼ yard	¼ yard	⅜ yard	⅜ yard
Ivory print	⅜ yard	⅜ yard	⅜ yard	⅜ yard	½ yard	½ yard
Medium-weight fusible interfacing	¾ yard	¾ yard	¾ yard	¾ yard	¾ yard	¾ yard
Additional supplies	Sweatshirt Other supplies listed on page 5 3 buttons, at least 1" in diameter					

cutting

From the large-scale floral, cut:

7 strips (or more, depending on sweatshirt size),
  3" x 42"

2½"-wide bias strips (enough to go around the jacket
  and sleeves, plus 10" for mitered corners and finishing, plus 18" for button loops—about 170" to 200").
  See "Binding" on page 6 for instructions on cutting
  the strips.

From the green floral, cut:

4 strips (or more, depending on sweatshirt size),
  3" x 42"

From the blue print, cut:

2 strips (or more, depending on sweatshirt size),
  3" x 42"

From the ivory print, cut:

3 strips (or more, depending on sweatshirt size),
  3" x 42"

sweatshirt preparation

Read the "General Instructions" on page 5 before
starting your project.

1. Follow the steps for "Deconstructing the Sweatshirt"
    on page 5. *Do not* cut the side seams. In step 4, cut
    off the shoulder seam allowances on the seam line,
    cutting straight through the neckband. *Do not* cut
    off the neckbands.

2. Lay the sweatshirt on a cutting table, front side up.
    To create a squared-off armhole opening, measure
    in 2" from one armhole edge at the shoulder and
    draw a vertical line down, stopping in line with
    the natural end of the armhole. Draw a horizon-
    tal line connecting this line to the side of the
    sweatshirt at the end of the armhole as shown in
    the illustration on page 30. Repeat for the other
    armhole. Cut along the newly marked armhole
    lines.

3. Follow the steps for "Interfacing and Prepping the Sweatshirt" on page 6. In step 1, on the right side of the sweatshirt, draw a vertical line on the left front straight down from the outermost point of the neckline to the lower edge. Draw a diagonal line from the outermost point on the right side of the neckline to where the left vertical line meets the lower edge of the sweatshirt as shown. Measure up from the lower edge of the sweatshirt the amount shown for your size and draw a new horizontal hemline. In step 3, cut along the new hemline first, through both layers, and then cut on the diagonal line to create the front opening, cutting through the front layer of the sweatshirt only.

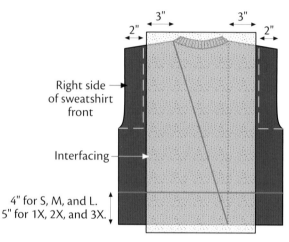

Mark the sweatshirt, apply interfacing, and cut on the solid marked lines.

quilting the front and back

1. Lay the sweatshirt on a flat surface, right side up. Cut a piece of large-scale floral on the crosswise grain to cover the sweatshirt back and fronts from the lower edge to 6" above the armhole opening.

2. Cover the sweatshirt with the fabric, placing the grain line in the fabric perpendicular to the lower edge, and pin the layers together with safety pins. Quilt over the floral fabric as desired.

3. Machine baste ¼" from the edges of the sweatshirt where it is covered with fabric and stay stitch around the armhole openings. Trim away the excess fabric.

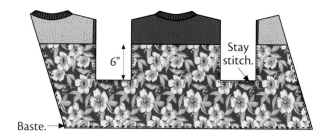

back and front tucks

1. Measure from the shoulder at the armhole edge down the back the amount shown for your size in the illustration after step 3; draw a horizontal placement line with chalk or a fabric pen for the first tuck. You should be drawing on the quilted fabric. Adjust placement if necessary.

2. Fold a 3" strip of green floral in half lengthwise; press. Place the strip on the sweatshirt with the raw edges of the fabric on the marked line. Sew ¼" from the raw edges, stretching the fabric slightly. Trim off the excess strip and reserve for later use. Repeat with a large-scale floral strip, only this time place the folded edge of the strip so it covers the sewing line of the previous strip by ¼". Continue in the same manner adding an ivory print strip, a large-scale floral strip, a blue print strip, and a large-scale floral strip, and then repeat in the same order until the remainder of the back is covered with strips.

3. Machine baste ¼" from the edges of the sweatshirt where it is covered with tucked fabric and stay stitch ¼" below the neckband. Trim away any excess fabric. Cut off and discard the back sweatshirt neckband.

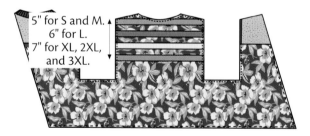

4. Add tuck strips to the left sweatshirt front section in the same manner as for the sweatshirt back and in the same order. Baste around the edges, trim the excess fabric, and cut away the front neckband in the same manner as for the back.

right front

Draw lines 1" apart following the diagonal edge of the right front. Add tuck strips to the front in the same manner as for the back and in the same order, following the marked diagonal lines and starting at the armhole edge.

sleeves and sleeve bands

1. Cut 1" off the bottom of each sleeve and discard. Cut a 4" strip off the bottom of each sleeve and square up the sides to make sleeve bands.

2. Make tuck strips and stitch them to the bands in the same manner as for the jacket back. Start with a green floral strip and align the fold in the strip with the lower edge of one of the bands. Stitch in place. Continue, adding an ivory print strip and a large-scale floral print strip. Repeat for the second band.

3. Find the center of the band and draw a vertical line 1" on either side. Continue drawing vertical lines 2" apart on both sides of the centerlines. Stitch on the marked lines to hold the tucks in place. Set the sleeve bands aside.

4. From the remaining large-scale floral, cut fabric to cover the two sleeves, cutting on the crosswise grain to match the direction of the pattern on the jacket. Lay the sweatshirt sleeves on a cutting table, right sides up. Cover the sleeves with fabric, aligning the grain line of the fabric with the center of the sleeves. Pin the layers together with safety pins and quilt in the same manner as for the jacket.

5. Machine baste ¼" from the edges of the sweatshirt sleeves and trim away the excess fabric.

6. Pin a band to the lower edge of a sleeve, right sides together, matching centers and easing as necessary. If the band is narrower than the lower sleeve width, taper the side edges of the sleeve from the outer edge of the band to the outer edges of the sleeve at the underarm. Stitch the band in place using a ¼" seam allowance. Press the seam allowances toward the sleeve. Measure the length of the horizontal edge of the armhole opening on the jacket and record. Fold the sleeve in half with right sides together and pin the long raw edges together. Stitch using a ¼" seam allowance, leaving an area unstitched at the end equal to one-half the recorded measurement of the horizontal edge of the armhole opening plus ¼" for the seam allowance. Press the seam allowances open and turn right side out.

Basting stitches →

Leave open.

shoulder seams

1. Pin the jacket front to the jacket back, right sides together at the shoulder seams, aligning the neck and armhole edges. If the shoulder widths are off a bit, align the edges at the armhole. The neckline edges can be trimmed later for a smooth transition.

2. Stitch the shoulders using a ½" seam allowance. Press the seam allowances open. Topstitch ¼" from the seam line on both sides. If the shoulder widths did not align at the neckline, trim them now.

attaching sleeves

1. Clip to the stay stitching at the corners of the armhole opening on the right side as shown. Mark the center of the horizontal edge with a pin.

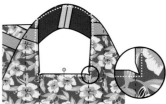

Clip corners of armhole.
Mark center with a pin.

2. Spread the unstitched area of the sleeve seam open and with right sides together, pin it to the horizontal edge of the jacket underarm, aligning the ¼" seam line at the end of the sleeve with the corner of the stay stitching on the armhole. Starting at the corner of the stay stitching, stitch ¼" from the raw edges and end when you reach the center pin mark. Repeat for the other side.

3. Pin the sleeve cap to the remainder of the armhole opening, matching the pin marks on the sleeves to the shoulder seams. Stitch ¼" from the raw edges, starting and ending stitching at the corners of the stay stitching. To reinforce the corners, start stitching 1" from the corner and stop at the corner with the needle down, rotate the sleeve, and continue stitching for 1" on the remaining side. Turn the jacket right side out.

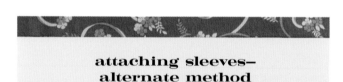

attaching sleeves— alternate method

If stitching a sleeve into a square corner makes you nervous, try the alternate method below. Follow steps 1 to 3 on pages 31 and 32, with the following exceptions:

• In step 1, do not clip to the stay stitching.

• In step 2, begin and end machine stitching ¼" from the corners of the stay stitching. Hand stitch the last ¼" on each side.

• In step 3, hand stitch the first ¼" around the armhole on each side and complete the remaining stitching by machine. Clip to the stay stitching at the corners when the sleeve is completely stitched in place.

finishing

1. Stitch three buttons to the left side of the jacket about 1" from the edge, placing the first button at the bottom of the last tuck. Space the remaining buttons about 4" apart.

2. Cut a 1¼" x 18" strip from binding. Press ¼" to the wrong side on the long edges of the binding. Fold the binding in half, wrong sides together, and stitch the long edges together by hand.

3. Fold the binding in half as shown to create the button loop. Position the loop on the jacket across from a button and check the length. Adjust the length as necessary and stitch the ends of the loop to the edge of the jacket as shown. Repeat for the remaining button loops.

4. Refer to the instructions for "Binding" on page 6 and bind the edges of the jacket, starting at the lower edge of the jacket back. Bind the edges of the sleeves.

The loop closures are added before the binding, permitting the loop ends to be concealed inside the binding during finishing. This method allows the loop closures to extend over both bound edges of the center front, creating a neat appearance.